I0815372

Gross Stuff!

Gross Stuff in Nature

by Julie Murray

Dash!
LEVELED READERS
An Imprint of Abdo Zoom • abdobooks.com

Level 1 – Beginning
Short and simple sentences with familiar words or patterns for children who are beginning to understand how letters and sounds go together.

Level 2 – Emerging
Longer words and sentences with more complex language patterns for readers who are practicing common words and letter sounds.

Level 3 – Transitional
More developed language and vocabulary for readers who are becoming more independent.

abdobooks.com

Published by Abdo Zoom, a division of ABDO, PO Box 398166, Minneapolis, Minnesota 55439.

Printed in the United States of America, North Mankato, Minnesota.
052025
092025

Photo Credits: Getty Images, Shutterstock
Production Contributors: Jennie Forsberg, Grace Hansen, John Hansen
Design Contributors: Candice Keimig, Neil Klinepier

Library of Congress Control Number: 2024947661

Publisher's Cataloging in Publication Data

Names: Murray, Julie, author.
Title: Gross stuff in nature / by Julie Murray
Description: Minneapolis, Minnesota : Abdo Zoom, 2026 | Series: Gross stuff! | Includes online resources and index.
Identifiers: ISBN 9781098288648 (lib. bdg.) | ISBN 9781098289348 (ebook) | ISBN 9781098289690 (Read-to-me ebook)
Subjects: LCSH: Cleanliness--Juvenile literature. | Ecological processes--Juvenile literature. | Microorganisms--Juvenile literature. | Nature--Juvenile literature. | Sanitation--Juvenile literature. | Curiosities and wonders--Juvenile literature.
Classification: DDC 591.5--dc23

Table of Contents

Gross Stuff in Nature

Being out in nature can be peaceful. Seeing beautiful plants and animals can bring a sense of well-being. But nature can also be pretty gross!

Invertebrates

Dung beetles roll fresh poop into balls. They eat it for food. They also lay their eggs on it. They can roll a ball that is 50 times their body weight.

Ticks are blood-eating bugs that feed on animals and humans. They attach themselves to a **host**. Then, they suck its blood. They can spread illnesses such as **Lyme disease**.

Earthworms dig through the soil and keep it healthy. But they are quite gross! Their long bodies are covered in **mucus**. The African giant earthworm can grow over 20 feet (6.1 m) long.

Maggots are the **larvae** of flies. They are found in **decaying** organic matter.

They feed on dead animals, animal poop, and rotting plants.

Bullet ants have large stingers and pinchers. They are named for the extreme pain they cause when they sting. The pain is compared to being shot by a bullet.

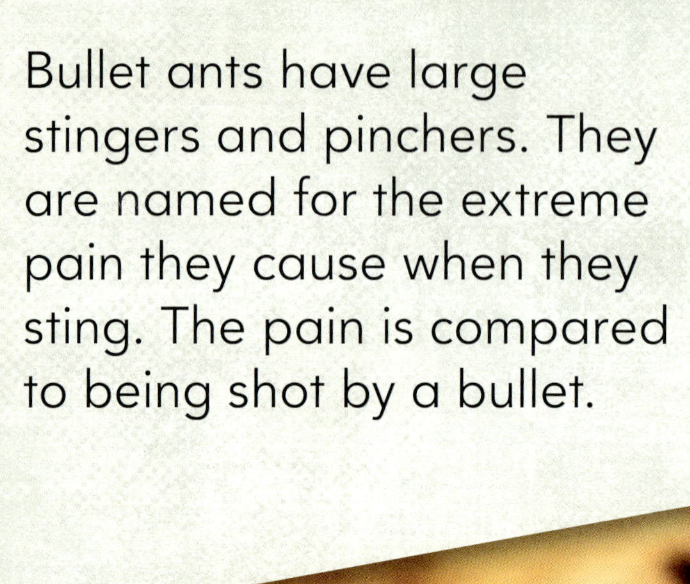

pinchers

Plants and Fungus

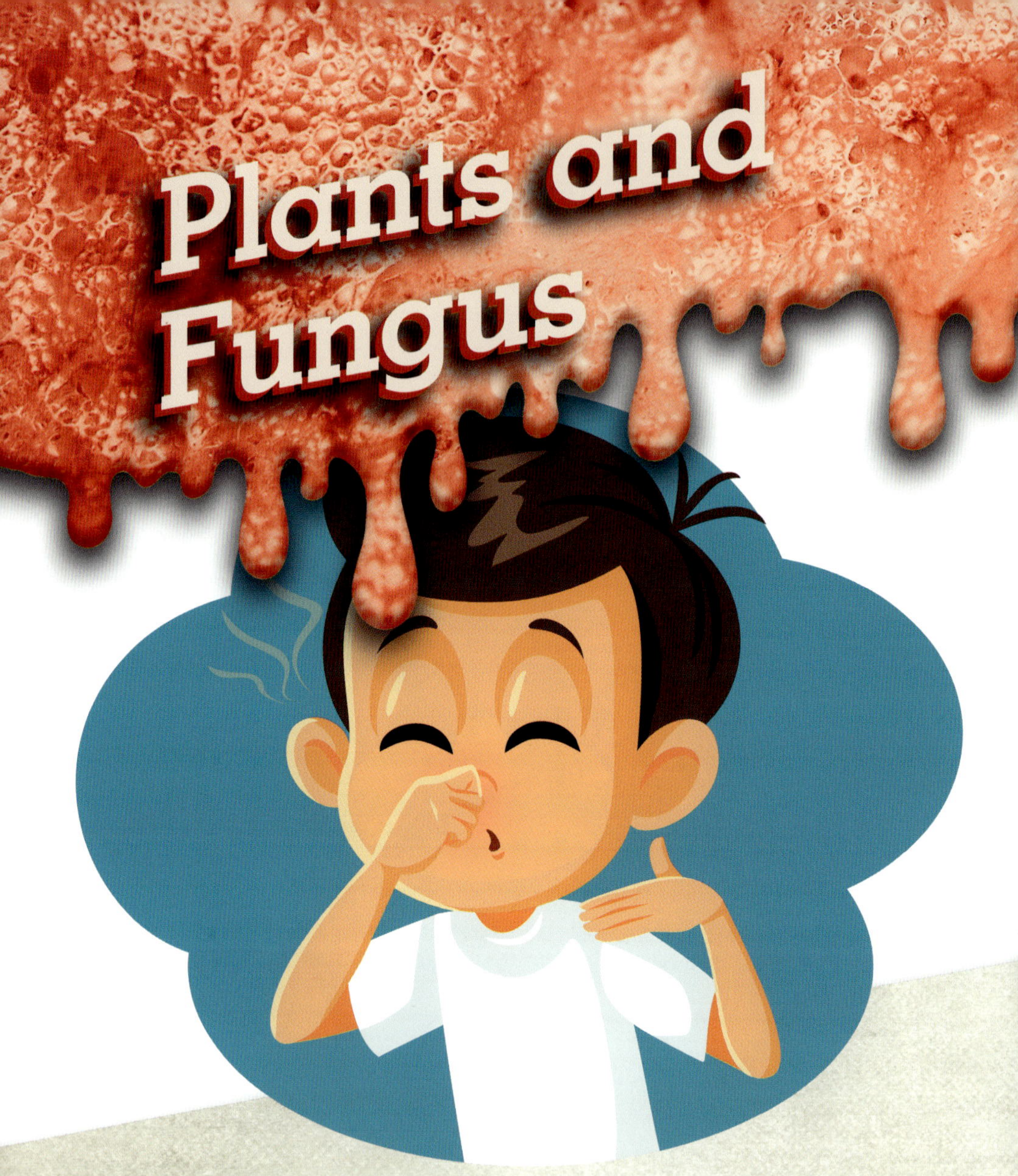

The corpse flower only blooms for a few days every two to three years. But when it blooms, it smells like rotting meat. Its smell can travel up to half a mile (0.8 km)!

The Venus flytrap is a **carnivorous** plant. Its leaves snap shut to trap its **prey**. It slowly breaks down its prey and takes it in. It eats ants, grasshoppers, and other insects.

Purple jellydisc is a common **fungus** found in nature. It grows in bunches on the trunks and branches of dead trees. It is a jellylike material that looks like a brain!

More Facts

- Centipedes have many body sections and legs. The Amazonian giant centipede can be more than 1 foot (0.3 m) long. It can have over 20 pairs of legs!

- The Burmese python can open its mouth more than 10 inches (25 cm) wide. It eats large animals such as deer and pigs. It can swallow them whole!

- The carrion plant can be found in the desert regions of Tanzania and South Africa. It smells like rotting flesh to attract flies to eat!

Glossary

carnivorous – eating the flesh of animals.

decaying – rotting.

fungus – one of a large group of living things that appear similar to plants but cannot make their own food using sunlight in the way plants do.

host – a plant or animal that parasites use to live on or in.

larva – an insect after it hatches from an egg and before it changes into its adult form.

Lyme disease – a serious disease passed to humans by certain ticks, which can cause fatigue, headache, joint pain, and other problems.

mucus – a slimy, slightly sticky material that coats and protects certain parts of the body.

prey – an animal that is hunted by other animals for food.

Index

Online Resources

To learn more about gross stuff in nature, please visit **abdobooklinks.com** or scan this QR code. These links are routinely monitored and updated to provide the most current information available.